LEADER

OF

LEADERS

Empowering Teacher Leaders to Produce
Leaders in Different Domains

DR. S. SMILEE BOSE

ISBN
Paperback 979-8-89475-601-1
Hardcase 979-8-89556-268-0

— Dedication —

This book is dedicated to my beloved *husband*...

Who listens attentively, inspires and encourages
me while I work hard, and makes me strong
enough to meet my cherished goals.

Acknowledgements

Every accomplishment in life is the result of teamwork. Considering that we are all a sum total of everything we have learned from all the people and experiences we have had in our life, no one can take entire credit for any measure of accomplishment in any endeavour. This book is no different. I want to thank the Almighty God for helping me to identify my gift as a teacher-leader and helping me to complete this book so that I can pass it on to generations to come.

I thank my beloved husband, Y. Dhinakaran, and my adorable daughter, D. Evangeline Evita, for their support, patience, and cooperation while I work on the numerous tasks that are part of my responsibilities on earth. I am grateful to them for enabling me to use my unique talent and allowing me to serve society.

Contents

Introduction 7

Chapter 1 – The Leader's Mindset....................................11

Chapter 2 – Identifying The Purpose 19

Chapter 3 – Taking Charge of Teacher Leadership.....................30

Chapter 4 – Qualities of a Teacher-Leader 39

Chapter 5 – Character – The Pioneering Quality
       in a Teacher-Leader...49

Chapter 6 – Teacher-Leader – a Teacher and a Cultivator 58

Chapter 7 – Be a Person of Values....................................64

Chapter 8 – The Art of Producing a Potential Leader 71

Introduction

Lack of teacher leadership in the society causes crisis in all the areas of the society.

—Dr. S. Smilee Bose

Leadership begins with your belief. Your belief system is the result of what you see, hear, and read. Hence, it is necessary to believe the truth because our beliefs become our ideas, and our ideas become our life philosophy. I personally had a strong conviction that 'leaders' are the people who rule us, who are in 'power' and 'position,' but when I came to know 'what leadership is,' my belief of seeing people in power and position changed. I started believing that 'all are born to lead.'

All the riches and power that we possess cannot make us leaders. The belief in ourselves will only make us a leader. We live in a world of uncertainty; we face different problems in society, such as immorality, economic uncertainty, social transformation, problems in politics, and problems in society. These conditions demand the highest quality of leadership, but the question is, "Do we have good leaders to manage these crises in society?" Nowadays, we come across people who claim themselves to be leaders who are merely corrupt and misuse authority, except the blessed few who are honest enough.

I believe that a true leader should live a life of standards. We are in desperate need of true leaders in all areas, like education, sports, politics, religion, medicine, economics, finance, etc. It is important to understand that the leadership of a teacher plays an important role in transforming society. People who are in power and positions in different fields were once the students of a dedicated and exceptional teacher, and this teacher need not be a professional teacher from an educational institution. It can be any personality, such as a mother, father, friends, relatives, etc. We are the sum total of what we learn. So, whatever we learn from the people around us influences us greatly! This book is dedicated to helping you to understand the importance of 'teacher as a leader.'

The Leader's Mindset

As a man thinks in his heart, so is he.
—King Solomon

What we think about ourselves determines who we are. Many of us do not believe that we are valuable, unique, and important, and this creates a philosophy in our mind that we are born to be a follower for a lifetime. Here, you must understand one thing: leadership is a hidden potential within each and every human. Our mindset is conditioned in such a way from our childhood that we are not born to lead. Only a selected group of people are born to lead. I believe it's a myth.

I would like to narrate a story so that you would understand how our mindset functions.

Once, there lived a farmer on a mountain who was taking care of his chickens. One fine morning, he went down the hills to his paddy field. On his way, he suddenly saw an egg lying on the ground near a tree. The farmer looked around and searched on the trees for any nest. He couldn't find anything, so he waited for a while and took the egg in his bag safely to his home. When he reached home, he put the egg together with the hen's eggs. After a few days, the egg hatched along with a few other eggs and grew among the hens. The farmer was surprised to know that it was an eagle, but the farmer decided to grow him in a chicken coop among his other chickens. The eagle grew up believing it was a chicken by doing what chickens do. One day, this eagle saw a huge bird flying high in the sky. The eagle was very impressed. The eagle asked the hens about that bird, and the hens replied it was the king of birds, the eagle. Then, the little eagle in the hen coop asked the hens if it could fly like this, and the chickens laughed and said, "Eagles are born to be in the sky, and we are born to be on the earth." The little eagle believed what the hens said and flew a short distance as chickens did. So, the eagle lived and died, believing that it was a chicken!

This story gives me a deep insight into leadership. I firmly believe that our conviction or our mindset plays a major role in understanding the true nature of leadership we possess. We believe that in our entire lifetime, we are born to follow and die as a follower. I used to think about the eagle in the story: if it had tried or come out of the safe confines of the chicken coop, it might have realised its true potential. We all possess the leadership spirit within us; to bring that out, we need to change our mindset. We must develop a belief that we are born to lead.

As teachers, we have a greater responsibility to lead the followers to cultivate leadership qualities and to help them bring out the hidden potential within them.

Believe You Are Born to Lead

Our life is what our thoughts make it

–Marcus Aurelius.

What you think about yourself determines your life or future. Whatever we sow, we will reap. So, if you plant a mango seed, you will reap it. After planting a mango seed, you cannot expect an orange. Likewise, if you plant negativity or failures, you will reap that; if you plant in your mind that you are a follower for a lifetime, you can only become a follower. When I was younger, I had a strong desire to pass on my knowledge to others. What I planted in my mind was, 'One day, I will become a teacher.' One day, it took place!

Now, as a teacher, I believe that a teacher could lead the students into leadership in different fields like education, sports, finance, architecture, medicine, engineering, entertainment, etc. A leader who can produce leaders in different areas is a teacher.

Our thoughts become our mindset. The way we behave, speak, and act is based on the ideas we have fed our minds. In order to capture the leadership mentality, we must look inside ourselves to examine how our beliefs affect our actions. In leadership, it's important to have a leadership mindset. Research shows that the most effective leaders have a strong mindset about their leadership capabilities. Effective leadership is the result of strong convictions and commitment to the principles and vision they believe in. Generally, people's concepts of their origin influence the way they think about themselves. People dare to think of themselves as leaders because their mindset about leadership is that 'leadership is reserved for the elite and chosen people.'

The one thing that I would like to highlight is that "We all live by our thoughts, and that, in turn, becomes our behaviour and is reflected in ourselves and others." There are many theories about leadership, but no matter what, you are born to lead. I will make it clear by stating an example. If anyone dominates us, we feel weird and question, 'Who is he or she to dominate me?' We respond to that situation by getting angry, frustrated, and depressed. Sometimes, we feel like adjusting to that situation because we think that those who are dominating are ruling over us. We believe that these kinds of people are true leaders. Don't come to the wrong conclusion that a leader is born to dominate other people; it's absolutely false. People are born with the finest spirit to lead in the areas of their special talents. This may be in different areas like teaching, dancing, singing, cooking, counselling, public speaking, or any other unique skill. Few people are gifted with one or two skills, and some have multiple skills; you need not worry about it. Identify your talent and work on it until you refine it.

As a teacher, you are gifted with the skill of developing people, i.e., your students. This is the most unique and outstanding gift of all! Teaching and transforming a person is not an easy task. It requires a lot of commitment and hard work. Nowadays, the teaching profession is considered an easy job, and whether the teacher possesses the art of teaching and developing a student is not prioritised. Anyone who owns a Ph.D. in any of the disciplines and qualifies in the eligibility examinations can either become a professor or a teacher and get appointed in any of the educational institutions. This kind of appointment spoils the students' careers, and the leadership skills die within the students as there is none to nurture or develop them. So, teachers, if you firmly believe that you are born to lead in the area of teaching, you also should believe that you are a 'leader' who would ultimately 'reshape' and 'mould' young minds and help them to become successful leaders in different areas of their special talents.

Most people do not believe that they are born to lead; they always lack confidence in themselves and regard their 'higher authorities' or 'heads' as their leaders. If you have the most influencing power to inspire and motivate others, you are certainly a good leader! For this, you do not need to own great titles or power. Changing your mindset and believing in your leadership power will help you to transform your students.

Have you seen eagles? These birds build their nests, called 'eyries,' on the top of hills or cliffs; when the eaglets are born, they remain in the nest for about 10 to 12 weeks. Once the eaglet is fully feathered enough to fly, the mother eagle will push the eaglet from the cliff. The eaglet has no clue about the new changing environment but is on the way to the ground, facing an uncertain and challenging situation. The eaglet begins to flap its wings without its knowledge. Flapping the wings helps the eaglet to stay in the air. It will do it again and again and finally understand that the hidden potential of flying lies within it. Likewise, when we start believing, we tend to meet difficult people and complex and challenging situations, but when we discover the true nature of leadership within us, it will help us to stay in the right positions as the eaglet in the air. So, until we change the mindset, nothing changes around us; unless a teacher has the leadership mentality, they cannot transfer it to their students.

You are born to lead but always learn and train yourself to become a leader in your area of skill. When your heart captures that you are born to lead, it will bring a transformation in thoughts and it will help you to become a perfect leader. Always remember that to become a leader, status, power, position or titles are not necessary. It's all about your mindset.

Inculcate a 'Do Not Wait' Mindset

Inculcate a "do not wait" mindset within you so that you can produce responsible citizens for the nation. Leaders don't wait for things to happen; they initiate change. Many people complained about slavery, but Mahatma Gandhi took the leadership to lead the nation towards freedom. Many poor people suffered in the streets of Calcutta; Mother Teresa took the leadership to help the lepers and the poor. Likewise, a teacher should initiate the change through the students in society. One who waits for instruction does not qualify to lead or produce leaders. So, when you desire to lead, take your position as a leader and bring changes in your students' lives. I have heard teachers saying that we need to work as per instructions; we don't have the freedom to express our ideas and views. Yes, sometimes it happens because we work together as a community to bring transformation in society or the nation, so we need to follow certain common principles for the betterment of the teachers and the organisation. But you can influence the students one hundred percent in your own class. Every day, you get a minimum of forty-five minutes with your class students; this is the golden hour in your hands to influence the students and transform their lives. So, never wait for instructions to transform your students; it's about your determination to go beyond the curriculum and teach life to the students.

Use Fertilisers for Your Mind

We come across different people with different backgrounds, ideas, and beliefs in our lives. It is necessary for us to understand what the truth is. If somebody is following something, it may not be necessarily true, so don't confuse yourself with what the majority of people are following around you. You need a good mindset to discern things around you before accepting them as the philosophy of life. To prepare your mind for that condition, you need to fertilise your mind. Fertile soil always yields good crops; likewise, a fertile mind yields good results. Soil is made fertile using manure, and other fertilisers are required in order to grow a particular crop; likewise, a mind needs to be conditioned using positive thoughts, learning the truth, and associating with people of high moral standards. A seed cannot grow in rocky fields; likewise, good thoughts, ideas, and creativity cannot be seen in a polluted mind. As a teacher-leader, you need to make your mind fertile in the right way to accept your leadership journey and the responsibilities attached to it.

> **Thought to Ponder**
>
> The one who identifies himself/herself
> as a true leader, never waits for instruction.

Identifying The Purpose

If you can't figure out your purpose, figure out your passion for your passion will lead you right into your purpose.

—Bishop T.D. Jakes

For thousands of years, researchers and philosophers have been trying to define or explore 'What is the purpose of life?' There are some factors that drive your life. Sometimes, these factors might control your life in your working environment, debts, family situation, etc. There may be many reasons which emotionally make you feel good or bad about yourself. For example, many people live their lives for others; their thoughts are always about social status, neighbours, friends, and colleagues. They want to live a life pleasing everyone and always expect someone to approve of them. If you are a person who lives on the opinion of others, then you are living below your potential without identifying your purpose. If you find your life's purpose, you will never live on other people's opinions. Teacher leadership is also a calling. If you are not called to teach, 'it's not your cup of tea' because you will not be in a position to create the next generation of leaders; it's not a job, it's a responsibility. I have talked with many teachers and asked them, 'Why did you choose a teaching career?' The answers will be 'It is the safest job, a noble profession, and status in society,' but only very few say that 'It's my passion.'

Many teachers nowadays pursue teaching by thinking of it as a job, not as a responsibility. Many teachers are busy doing the wrong thing; they may be good at completing the given task, but bringing transformation into the lives of the students can only be done by teachers whose purpose is to teach. If a teacher wants to know who they are in order to live and deliver their gifts in the right way, they must first understand the purpose of teaching and the heart of teacher leadership. The only leadership area where followers are directly transformed into leaders is 'teacher leadership.' Every one of us in this world has only one life, and it's our responsibility to make life useful to fulfil our purpose. How are we using our lives? What value do we place in our lives? Do we know that one of the most dangerous things in life is wasting time? Once you've lost time, it's gone forever. What you've lived, you can never relive. So, the best thing to do with time is to use it in a way that will bring the greatest results. The best way to use time effectively is to do what you were born for. Suppose you have found out that your purpose of existence in this world is to teach others to make use of every opportunity. Don't just teach to make a living. That's not fulfilling your purpose. Fulfilling your teaching purpose is doing it from your heart for the betterment of your students. Effectiveness does not mean just doing good things but rather doing the right things.

Most of us are not interested in discovering what we can accomplish when we go to our jobs. We go to work only because we want a paycheque. If you have not identified your purpose, you are abusing the talents and gifts that the creator has put in you.

Busy Doing the Wrong Thing

It is important to identify the purpose before planning. The greatest mistake human beings make in their lives is being busy doing the wrong things their entire lives. Wouldn't it be sad to be seriously committed and faithful to the wrong things? It's possible to do what is good but not what is right. The danger in teacher leadership is getting busy with things that are good but not what is right.

A teacher was busy with file work, 'Is that good?' 'Yes'; a teacher is busy collecting fees and dues, 'Is that good?' 'Yes, of course,' but 'Do you think it is right?' Everything is good, but 'Is it the right work for the teacher-leader who is responsible for transforming or leading the future generation?' Everything in this world has a purpose — teaching has a purpose, learning has a purpose, teachers have a purpose, learners have a purpose — but when the purpose of a thing is not known, abuse is inevitable.

The only way to live a fulfilled life is to know 'why we are born.' Have you ever had an experience of your new mobile phone not working when you want to make an urgent call? You must have dropped your phone on your table, chair, or sofa with great anger. You just wanted to yell at it because it did not fulfil its purpose. It was a brand-new one. It looked sleek, and it had a nice fancy look, but you couldn't use it. What made you angry at the mobile phone? It's simple: the mobile's purpose was to connect you with others, but the mobile was not taking you anywhere. No matter how great the mobile looked, it didn't fulfil its purpose. Many people are like mobile phones. They're stopped in the middle of a call, and they don't even realise it. They are spending their lives doing things that look good; knowing and fulfilling your purpose is the only way to do what is right. Finding our purpose helps us stop wasting time and start living up to our full potential. However, we must be careful not to become sidetracked along the way.

The greatest way to destroy someone is to distract the person from his or her true purpose. Reinforce your purpose. I can't emphasise strongly enough that knowing your purpose is crucial for your life's course. I know it's not easy to take a hard look at yourself, but it's necessary if you're going to discover your true purpose in life. You will be busy doing meaningful work when you learn 'why you are here.' Don't give up on having a purposeful life, no matter what your age is. Get busy with the right things.

Outcome of a Purpose-Driven Life

Your Life Gives Meaning to You and Others

When the purpose is discovered, the life you live takes on new meaning. If you live a life without purpose, you live a meaningless life. If a mango tree produces watermelons, it's evident that the mango tree didn't accomplish its purpose; the purpose of a mango tree is not to produce any other fruits; its purpose is to produce what it is created for. The same principle that is found in nature is applicable to our lives as well. Nobody will be interested in plucking a watermelon from a mango tree.

Similarly, our followers can never be influenced by the meaningless life we live. The life which we live should be lived on what we are called for. Many times, we feel happy that we are doing something which is good but whether it is right or not is a big question. In order to make your life and your followers' lives meaningful, you need to explore the purpose for which you are made. This can be explored only by having a good relationship with your creator.

It Gives a Quality to Your Life

There should be a reason for waking up every day. When you know what your purpose is, the quality of your life improves. You choose your environment based on your purpose, you choose your career based on your purpose, you choose your friends based on your purpose, you choose the books you read based on your purpose, and you choose your lifestyle based on the purpose of your life. So, your life transforms when the purpose is identified. When your life is transformed, it's easy to transform your followers. A leader should live a standard life to lead the followers to a quality life.

Disciplines Your Life

When the purpose is known, we will not waste resources, we will not abuse our lives, and we will never waste the greatest resource — time. Time is a unique and valuable resource given to every individual on earth. It plays a very important role in our lives. The right use of time reduces stress and anxiety and enables us to achieve our goals faster. Time is limited, impalpable, and fleeting. The one who makes effective use of it reaps the benefit; using time effectively is one of the important disciplines that need to be developed in everyone's life because when time is managed effectively, you learn self-discipline. Time can be managed and used effectively by people who know their purpose. If a person does not identify his or her purpose, they will have to live their life for others' purposes, which in turn wears them out in the long run.

Focus in Life

Focus is important for success; we all strive in our lives to become successful, but many of us are clueless about how to achieve success in what we do. This is the result of an unexplored purpose. When we identify our purpose, we can live a focused life. Our focus will be based on the purpose. For example, if our purpose is to teach, then we will concentrate on things that help us to develop our skills. Moreover, we often update ourselves by attending skill development courses and trying to create interesting factors to keep teaching interesting. When our purpose is not teaching, you cannot focus on connecting with your skills, and you will feel stressed and frustrated while doing it.

The Outcome of a Haphazard Life

When a life is lived with purpose, we start living our life to the fullest; it doesn't mean that we will not face any setbacks, failures, or depression. Every trouble we face in life makes us stronger and more valuable in accomplishing our life mission easily when we are committed and focused. The purpose will keep us alive, but when we do not know who we are, what we are doing, or where we are travelling in life, we live an aimless life. A teacher-leader can never live a haphazard or unfocused life because they are in a greater position to lead the students into leadership. If a teacher-leader is aimless, the student followers will suffer to identify their real potential.

Nowadays, students are studious, and they learn by themselves. They are exposed to different media to gain their knowledge, but they need a leader to help them apply their knowledge and use their abilities in the right way. Student followers fall into the age category, where they are easily misled. A teacher-leader should live a purposeful life. To be a leader, your followers should respect you for who you are. Many students do not respect the teachers because they feel they have less knowledge, they lack communication skills, and they do not live up to the standards. So, being a teacher-leader is not an easy task. Thus, it is necessary to live a life with purpose.

The Following Will Be the Outcome of a Haphazard or Aimless Life:

Lack of Self-discipline

Discipline is an important entity for any human being on earth. It's not an exception with teacher leaders. When the purpose of your life is not accomplished, you might take your work for granted. Self-discipline is the result of a purposeful life. When the purpose of teaching is not known by the teacher, they do teaching as a routine job for a monthly paycheque.

Nothing is free in this world, and everything costs something. I am not saying you should not get a paycheque; your hard work should be rewarded, but that alone should not be the focus for a teacher-leader because their purpose or their calling is to transform lives. Their involvement in updating themselves and making themselves valuable each day to serve their gift requires a lot of discipline. So, as a teacher-leader, if you have identified your area of gifting, you will never lack self-discipline.

Unrighteousness

Unrighteousness is not standing in the right position with the principles and statutes of life. There are certain moral values a teacher should possess. We have discussed this in detail under the topic 'Character.'

Fear

Fear is the result of self-ignorance. When people are not aware of themselves, they always live in fear; they worry about other people's opinions, they will live below their potential. When a teacher is not aware of his/her purpose, they live below their potential and they just follow others; they don't believe in their capabilities and creativity.

Fear will consume their ability to become what they are without their knowledge. So, identifying and living a purposeful life will help you to come out of fear. An unfocused life or a life without purpose will lead to a haphazard life.

Procrastination

When we do not know what to do or when we do not understand how important our life is, how important our work is, or the purpose of the work we are doing, there are chances we often procrastinate our duties and responsibilities. Knowing the importance and the purpose of what we do will help us perform to the fullest. Procrastinating is not a good act of any leader. So, as a teacher-leader, explore your purpose and never delay performing your duties.

Distractions

Distractions are everywhere around us. When we have not identified our purpose, it's easy for us to get distracted easily. Each and every day we get up to live a purposeful life; if we have not identified that, television will distract us, mobile phones will distract us, social networks will distract us, our friends will distract us, our family will distract us, and even our students will distract us from what we are supposed to do. We might not achieve everything that we want in life.

A teacher-leader should be cautious enough to understand the environment to lead the future generation into leadership. So, if a leader lives a haphazard life, everything around them will distract them from their responsibilities.

Thought to Ponder

When purpose is unknown it will be difficult to live to your potential.

Taking Charge of Teacher Leadership

Hold yourself responsible for a higher standard than anybody expects of you.
Never excuse yourself.

–Henry Ward Beecher

The command given to the disciples by Jesus Christ is: "Go and make disciples of all nations, teaching them the things I have taught you (Matthew 28:19–20)." Jesus asked his disciples to go and teach what they had learned. Many of us know many things, but "Are we willing to share with others to make them better?" The world is filled with ignorance. The teacher's main motto is to take the ignorance away from each student and bring light into their lives. For this, what you need to do is to take charge of teacher leadership. When I say to you, "You are a leader." The first thing that comes to your mind is that you are not a leader. You are an ordinary person or an ordinary teacher. You are not alone.

The vast majority of individuals do not think they are leaders, possess leadership qualities, or are even capable of rising to positions of leadership. Always believe you were born to lead. You have leadership potential trapped within you. The family background and the cultural environment have made us think in a way that we are not born to lead. All cultures around the world have different belief systems, which become their lifestyle. Few cultures teach people to remain followers throughout their lives. When I meet people who think they cannot be leaders, I tell them that they can, they must, and they should because they have the potential inside them. The only thing is that they are ignorant about themselves. The first step towards becoming a leader is to believe in their own leadership abilities. There are millions of stars in the galaxy, each one of which is unique and has its own brightness and radiance. Similarly, each human is unique and has their own brightness, but the opinion of others and doubt about your own radiance keep you away from leadership. You need to discover your area of gifting to take charge as a teacher-leader. A teacher-leader is born when you discover your gift of teaching. Finding your excitement and passion for teaching will help you to take charge as a teacher-leader. This requires a process of self-discovery. Teacher leadership is a gift from God.

Teacher leaders involve themselves in passing their knowledge to generations and making them better leaders. Before taking charge of leadership, teacher leaders should refine their gifts to make themselves and their students valuable to society. When you are known for your gift, the world will come to you for it. My passion is teacher leadership. I have devoted much of my life to studying teacher leadership. I live to teach and to share ideas that make student followers discover who they are, what their value is, what their worth is, what they can do, what they can achieve, and what they can become. In my opinion, the ultimate thing we can do for our students is to help them become the best they can become and to have a life where they can do more with their gifts.

What is the Price?

Teacher leadership demands a high price. If you check with teacher leaders who are successful and have produced successful leaders in life, they must have paid a higher price compared to others. The price we need to pay depends upon the area of leadership. When it comes to teacher leadership, the price we need to pay is one. Self-denial, two. Rejection, 3. Criticism, four. Loneliness, 5. Pressure.

TAKING CHARGE AS A SERVANT LEADER

What is teacher leadership? It is, above all, a service. A teacher-leader is a servant of the students. Jesus Christ taught his disciples, "If anyone wants to be first, he must be the very last and the servant of all." How do you become a teacher-leader by serving? Simple. You have to serve something valuable to your students. What do you serve? You have your gift. The gift of transferring knowledge and understanding. When you find your gift, and you serve it to the world of students, you become great. Having others serve you does not make you great. Teacher leadership is more about unleashing and deploying oneself for the benefit of one's students. Whatever your life's gift is, it is not yours to keep; it is yours to share with the rest of the world. God gave it to you. Please pass it on. Teacher leadership is serving your gift at every opportunity.

Teacher leadership is self-distribution to your generation. Stop waiting until you are great to start serving. Do not put it off until you get your degree, title, or promotion. Teacher leadership is becoming yourself for the benefit of your students. Teacher leadership is not something you do; it is something you become. You have to find out what you were born to become. That is your area of domain. Becoming yourself is a process that begins with self-discovery. If you are ready to take the journey, ask yourself: Am I really who I am? Take charge today as a teacher-leader and serve the students for a better generation tomorrow.

In Charge of the Right Area

Sometimes, at work, you might wonder, "Why isn't this working?" That's because it's not your area of talent. If you're tired, frustrated, and depressed from teaching and dealing with students, you're not the right person for the job. You are in places prepared for someone else. To know the right place for you, you must know your areas of gifting. You may not even know it. Sometimes your leaders may reveal it to you, sometimes you yourself will discover it, and sometimes your parents identify it. From history, we can identify how leaders in the wrong spot affect everyone around them. An example is Jonah. He was given directions by God to meet the people of Nineveh, but he chose another spot to be comfortable, took a ticket to Tarshish, and boarded a ship. Because of his wrong spot, everyone on the ship suffered the consequences. God sent a great storm that struck the ship, and the people on the ship decided to throw Jonah into the sea as the lot cast fell on the name of Jonah. When you are out of position, you affect other people. So, if you want to be a teacher-leader, you need to make sure you're in the right position, place, or spot before you choose teaching as a career. Please think again about whether teaching is your calling or where your gifts lie because your attitude will ruin the students.

Before You Take Charge of Teacher Leadership, Know This:

Teacher leaders will bring change into society.

Teacher leaders have a great ability to bring change in society. Dr A.P.J. Abdul Kalam, the former president of India, was a great teacher and scientist. He had a strong desire to transform young minds, and as president, he visited students directly, encouraging them to dream big and work hard. This had a significant impact on the students. Similarly, Anne Sullivan, the teacher of Helen Keller, proved through her innovative teaching that disability is not a hurdle to reaching one's destination. Helen Keller, in turn, served society by writing books and being an activist for various social causes. She made a significant impact on the disability community, inspired by her teacher, Anne Sullivan. History has produced many teachers who have made a profound impact on society. If other teacher leaders can bring about change, why can't we? As a teacher-leader, strive every moment for the betterment of your students. This will bring about a profound change in society.

Teacher Leaders Should Be a Model and a Mentor.

Unfair and unequal treatment is not part of a virtuous teacher-leader. Students are influenced by our speech and actions, so it is important that, as teacher leaders, you live an upright life.

Students watch teachers closely. In my life, I have experienced many teachers influencing me as a student in school or college. The way they behave, speak, dress, carry themselves, and treat people has influenced me a lot. Many things I follow in my life are what I learned from my teachers through their virtuous behaviour, as they were good role models. Many teachers have also been good mentors and provided their insights and knowledge, helping to shape my studies and career.

So, my dear teacher leaders, don't do anything just to please others. Whatever you do, do it from your heart and do it consistently so that you can influence many student disciples and bring a great change in their lives. They will never forget you for what you have done for them, directly or indirectly.

Teacher Leadership Is the Highest Calling to Commit Yourself to the Essence of Your Students' Lives and Their Noble Values.

Commitment to what we do makes us successful in our work. All teacher leaders desire success, and none of us want to fail. If we realise that teaching is the highest calling, which carries significant responsibility and accountability, we will commit ourselves to the betterment of our students. It's not about encouraging them only when we feel enthusiastic and then avoiding them when we don't feel good. Our support should be constant. Always be available for your students. Every moment spent with them in the classroom is an investment in their lives. Make every minute count and add value to their lives. When we, as teacher leaders, understand and acknowledge our higher calling, it will be fruitful for the students.

Teacher Leaders Never Oppress Students; They Liberate Them.

The role of a teacher remains profoundly impactful, capable of transforming society through leadership and guidance. During my teaching career, I encountered a student who was consistently angry and rude towards teachers. One day in my class, he sat quietly with his head down, ignoring my instructions to pay attention and take notes. Despite repeatedly asking him to engage, he remained unresponsive. Frustrated, I called his name loudly, but he still didn't respond. This behaviour persisted for nearly a week. Concerned, I decided to contact his parents. After obtaining his father's contact number from the class teacher, I called and explained the situation in detail. To my shock, his father revealed that the student's father had committed suicide two years ago, a tragedy that had deeply affected the boy.

Realising the impact of this trauma, my approach towards him changed. I began to pay special attention to him, speaking gently and offering support. Over the next semester, I noticed a remarkable transformation. The student started mingling with classmates and engaging positively with teachers.

This experience reinforced the nobility of our profession. As teacher leaders, it is crucial to look beyond surface behaviours and understand the underlying struggles our students may be facing. Labelling students as useless or stubborn can oppress them, while identifying and addressing their pain can liberate them. By monitoring and paying close attention to our students, we can make them feel supported and mentored, fostering an environment of growth and understanding.

Teacher Leaders Never Hurt Students; They Heal Them.

Students are like clay in the potter's hand. Just as clay is flexible to the potter's ideas and designs, students are mouldable in the teacher's hand. A teacher has the responsibility to shape students into good individuals. As a teacher-leader, you are the designer of a student's future. You should never hurt a student or leave any permanent scars in their life. Teachers should be supportive and caring and act as a remedy for all their mental and academic issues. Personal counselling can also be provided to students when needed. So, as a teacher-leader, never hurt your students. They are like clay in the potter's hand. If the potter does not give enough care and attention while making a pot, the mistakes will be evident in the finished product. So, be kind to your students. Let them always remember you for the role you played in their lives.

Thought to Ponder

When you have a firm grasp on what is most important to you, decision-making is a breeze.

Qualities of a Teacher-Leader

The growth and development of people is the highest calling of leadership.

—Harvey S. Firestone

As a teacher-leader, you should follow certain principles and values that would help the students to learn from you. Principles guarantee success; if you want to be successful, follow the principles. A principle is a law that works for anyone, anytime, and anywhere. When we live by principles, it's easy for us to influence others. As discussed earlier, we are conditioned from childhood that only a few people are born to lead or that people who are in power and position are born to lead. When you come out of this kind of stigma, your mentality and ideas change. When your ideas change, a transformation takes place within you, which helps you to understand the principles to be followed to become a great leader. As a teacher, you are born to lead and transform the students into great leaders for social betterment. So, you must be committed to certain principles and values to create leaders.

Vision

Any person with a vision can live a focused life. It helps the leader to see the future. Any visionary leader with a vision does not live in the present but lives in the future. The vision in teacher leadership produces visionary leaders for society. When the teacher-leader has a vision to lead the students into leadership, their lives are much more focused and disciplined, and their priorities will be based on their vision. The greatest king of Israel, King Solomon, says, "Where there is no vision, people perish." So, as a teacher, when you lead a group of students without any vision, the followers perish. A teacher-leader should not be a daydreamer but rather a person who acts on his/her vision.

Wisdom

Wisdom is divine; as King Solomon says, "Wisdom is supreme; therefore, get wisdom. Though it cost all you have, get understanding." Knowledge is the information we gain through our education, learning, hearing, and reading, but if you want to become wise, you need to have enough understanding about what you have learned, read, or heard. After that, you need to apply your knowledge and understanding in your real life. This application of knowledge is known as 'wisdom.' So, spend some money to get enough knowledge and understanding so that you can be a wise leader and lead your students into leadership.

Positive Attitude

Attitude helps us either to become successful or to meet failure in life. Leaders with a positive attitude are always confident about who they are and inspire others to do their best. Optimistic leaders communicate well, are self-disciplined and possess good time management skills, have a clear vision and never feel proud about the position they hold, and they look forward to life with courage, confidence, and contentment.

Self-Discipline

Self-discipline is an inherent skill which helps a person to strategise his/her goals in their life. A person can prioritise all the important tasks in their lives if they follow self-discipline. The development of self-discipline leads one to avoid acting on impulse, overcome procrastination and laziness, and concentrate/focus on one's work without losing focus on it. Self-discipline helps one to achieve his/her dreams. In today's world, people who make their dreams and goals outnumber people who are pessimistic by nature. A person cannot achieve success or receive the outcome without self-discipline. It helps one to achieve maximum potential in life.

Creativeness

Teacher leadership is always manifested in a creative way. The much-required quality of a teacher-leader is to be a creative leader. This creativeness in a teacher-leader will help the student followers see the unseen. Creative leaders never live in their past; they learn from the past and apply the experiences to future needs, combining the past and the present. The capacity for creating new things helps the student followers to think outside the box when they come across changes or crises in their lives as well as in society. When a teacher leaves the comfort zone and ventures into the uncomfortable zone that nobody else has reached, creativity is born.

Responsibility

A true teacher-leader always possesses a sense of responsibility. Each teacher-leader should be committed to himself/herself first; this is a great responsibility that leaders have towards themselves. Always keep in mind that you are responsible for your students' lives. Moreover, you are accountable to your higher authority. Being conscious of your responsibility as a teacher-leader will help you produce good results in your career.

Role Model

If you do not follow what you teach, you are not a good leader or a teacher. Generally, teachers are good at giving advice, but whether they follow it in their life is a question. Always remember we can influence people or make people believe us through the standards to which we are committed in life. So, remember that when you set a standard, you follow it first, then teach the students.

A true leader will always stay grounded in his/her principles. When you teach your students discipline, you first follow it. When you ask your students to come to class on time, you must be on time. I would like to share a true incident that happened in one of the institutions where I worked as a teacher. One day, while engaging in class, I saw a student sleeping inside the classroom, and the teacher threw a piece of chalk at him to wake him up and scolded him for sleeping inside the classroom. The student felt embarrassed and started crying. Then the teacher started advising the whole class that the students were inside the classroom to study and not to sleep and that they should know their responsibilities inside the classroom and follow the decorum of the class. The student realised the mistake and regretted sleeping during class hours. After this incident, the student amended the mistake and maintained good decorum during class hours.

After a few months, one day, the student passed by the teacher's cabin, where the teacher was sound asleep during working hours. This student started recollecting the past incident and immediately wrote a note to the teacher and left it on the teacher's table. As soon as the teacher woke up, she read the note, and it said, "Don't sleep during working hours; maintain decorum inside the campus." The teacher was embarrassed, and she realised her mistake. The result is that the student had a bad impression of the teacher, and the teacher failed to inspire the student by breaking down the standards she herself had set for the students. So, always stay committed to your standards before setting them for others. Teach what you follow for great leadership.

Serve Others

Leadership is all about serving others; it's not about people serving the leader. In our society, we have a misconception that leaders should be served. It's a myth. The leadership, the title, and the position they hold is to serve others. So, when you are a 'Leader,' serve your followers. This will make you and your followers great. As a teacher-leader, have a serving mindset and focus on empowering and uplifting your students. Always look for the possibilities to bring out the potential of the students and empower them. This will help the students reach the desired destination in their lives.

Don't be an overseer, and try to manage your students as a leader; try to develop them by serving gifts. Teach them what you know, teach them life's principles, teach them the truth, and teach them how to handle difficulties in life. If you start serving your students through your gifts, your students will benefit from it throughout their lifetime.

Good Communicator

"The leaders who know how to communicate their ideas clearly and make others understand are not only good leaders but great teachers." Teachers should be in a position to communicate well with the students so that their ideas can be inculcated in the students. Always make sure that your ideas are not facts but truth. In order to teach effectively, you need to develop yourself through attending workshops, seminars, training, orientations, reading, studying, and preparing. So, any knowledge that you gain first should be understood properly and then taught to the students so that it becomes effective teaching. Unless you understand what you have learned, you cannot make the students understand. Communication helps to clear the air between the communicator and the receiver, so a teacher should possess good and effective communication skills to inculcate true knowledge in the student.

One day the student of yours will become a leader, so always keep in mind you are creating leaders to lead in different areas in society. So, your ideas and concepts must be pure and true.

Always check what you teach to a group of students, and ensure whether it is true because they carry it for a lifetime.

Ethical/Moral Behaviour

Ethics are the firm principles and values that a leader should possess. Ethical behaviours are the principles on which leaders stand firmly. As teacher leaders, we are in a position to teach what is good and right. Moreover, it's our duty to follow it in our lifetime as a teacher. Every person should practice ethical behaviour, which is true. Many leaders set principles based on their beliefs and customs that may go wrong on many occasions, e.g., marrying the same gender may be ethical for someone, but the truth is it is against the nature of creation. So, as teacher-leaders, we should unlearn the lies and learn the truth for our sake as well as our followers' sake.

In teacher leadership, ethical behaviour is of utmost importance. There should be no complaint against the morality and righteousness of the leader. An ethical leader should stick to ethics and never compromise on his/her principles. There are times when we are compelled to be biased among students because they come from a political background or elite group of society. Stay firm on your feet and try to make them understand how it's going to affect their moral behaviour in the future. Don't run away from people who are immoral; rather, influence them by the way of your living. The remarkable virtues of ethicality should be understood by the leader as well as the follower to achieve the target.

Not Violent, but Gentle

A teacher should not handle their students violently. Whatever problems arise inside the classroom, they should be handled gently. A leader should not be aggressive but rather, with much care and wisdom, should build their character and change their attitude and behaviour. All the students are good, but only their circumstances make them behave differently from others. Teach them when they are wrong, and help them in renewing their mind and thoughts.

Trustworthy

You cannot lead students without gaining their trust. If the students do not trust you, they will ignore you. They will not give proper respect, and they will never follow your teaching. Be it any kind of relationship, once the trust is broken, it will be very hard to set it right and bring it back to normalcy. As great leaders, the teachers must be worthy of students' trust.

As a teacher-leader, you will have different tests, such as the test of reliability, test of consistency, test of character, test of truthfulness, and so on. Maintain your integrity at any cost for the sake of your students who are following you. Don't set a bad example by not being truthful. When the character in you is pure, the students can be influenced through that, either directly or indirectly. So set your standards high and never compromise on your standards. This will help you to maintain a good relationship with the students.

Thought to Ponder

The fact that you worry about being a good teacher, means that you already are one.

—Jodi Picoult

Character – The Pioneering Quality in a Teacher-Leader

Character, in the long run, is the decisive factor in the life of an individual and of nations alike.

—Theodore Roosevelt

Character is the most powerful force leaders can possess because it protects their life, leadership, and legacy. It manifests who they are and shapes who they will become. Leadership is at risk when the characteristics of the leaders are not good enough. Character is the most important quality in leadership because it protects and preserves your leadership. This character should start with your inner life. You must be pure from the inside to influence your outer circle; your personal character is more important than your external behaviours. You may be nice to everyone; you may pretend as if you are working, but if your inner character is rotten, it will be revealed one day in your leadership.

Teachers are great leaders in this world. Without teachers, no leaders can be formed. So, the characteristics of a teacher should be pure to influence the students since their position has a direct impact and a lasting effect on the students' lives. Living a moral and ideal life will not protect or prevent you from various life problems. Like everybody else, you would also experience struggles and setbacks in life. To be a successful teacher, you should possess good moral values in life. In day-to-day life, we hear news about leaders who are removed from their titles and positions because of bad character. If a leader possesses bad characteristics, it will not help the person to bring the true ability they possess to serve their gifts. Teachers with no moral values cannot teach a student to become a person of values. All of the titles we have, like teachers, mentors, and trainers, come from the students who have learned from us. When a teacher violates these moral values, they misuse the privilege given by their students. As a teacher, you fail to play the role of a leader to your student followers.

Many teacher leaders nowadays have a perception that without good characteristics, they cannot continue to be leaders in their area of leadership. This is the result of their mental conditioning because they think the only responsibility of a teacher is to teach the curriculum, and they forget that the student gets inspired or influenced by their character and moral values. Teacher leadership has the potential to transform a student's life completely. I have watched many teachers who have an excellent gift of teaching and making the students understand the lessons but compromise on moral values, e.g., teachers delegating their work to the students, teachers who smoke, teachers with immoral relationships, teachers who abuse students, etc., which have a detrimental effect on the students. Teachers should reconstruct and mend themselves before leading a group of students.

Your character will keep the leadership quality alive, not your titles and your education. Your teacher's leadership is validated by your character. So, when you don't possess good character traits, the leadership is at great risk. Your skills, your ability, or your potential as a teacher-leader will survive only when the character is pure. So, while leaders have many opportunities to use their talents and skills, it is their character that ultimately determines the effectiveness of their leadership.

One of my teachers told me that whatever you gain through compromising your principles will never stay with you for a long time. Many teacher leaders have sacrificed a great future by compromising their character for things that are not permanent. Many teachers have high potential, but they take their skills for granted and compromise them for temporary pleasure. Compromising their character does not make them qualify to lead the student followers to leadership. If an unethical leader leads a follower, 'What will be the result?' 'What will be the future of a society or a nation?' A teacher-leader can lead student followers only as far as they have gone themselves. And many of our teacher leaders have not stepped up to the starting line of character development, much less crossed it.

A future that includes strong, ethical leaders in our governments, businesses, educational institutions, civil organisations, and homes will be secured only by returning to character training and personal character development as our priority. A teacher-leader must embrace this challenge and actively seek to change their ways. Only then will our nation be uplifted from a mindset of corruption and compromise to an outlook of conviction and character? Instead of seeking political power, economic power, entertainment power, or sports power, leaders should pursue political character, economic character, entertainment character, or sports character. It's the core responsibility of a teacher-leader to produce leaders in our governing institutions, our communities, our businesses, our places of employment, and our families.

Leadership that is weak in ethics and values has allowed nations to fall apart. It has also initiated many of the problems we grapple with in the world. A return to integrity in leadership will enable us to confront these issues from a position of strength, determination, and honour. Many leaders whom we witness in society are educated on how to manage resources, but they were never taught how to live a valuable life or how to manage their own lives and how their application of such knowledge was crucial for effective and successful leadership. Each of us, as teacher leaders, must not only understand and implement the principles of leadership but also make a commitment to become established in character and adhere to a strong code of ethics. Then, we must continually grow in the development of our character so that we can have a positive and lasting impact on our student followers.

TEACHER-LEADER AS AN INFLUENCER

A good teacher can influence the students in the following ways:

Teacher leaders will influence the students.

Teachers can bring transformation in the minds of the students by influencing them to change their perspective from the way they previously behaved or acted or thought. When a teacher's focus is on changing the mindset of the student, obviously the character of the student will change. A teacher can influence the younger minds through different skills to make them identify what seems to be good or bad and what seems to be their comfort zone.

The beliefs, values, customs, and culture play an important role in conditioning a person's mindset. So, in order to influence the students and change their mindset, understanding and altering their values and beliefs is essential. Changing the mindset and making the students' progress towards positivity and truthfulness is the greatest gift a teacher can give to the students. Dr. A.P.J Abdul Kalam, the former president of India, understood that teachers play an important role in influencing the future of the students because his teacher, Shri Siva Subramania Iyer, was the one who taught Kalam "how birds fly," which influenced him to determine his career to become the 'Missile Man of India.' A positive influence has created an immeasurable impact on Kalam's life; this is the best gift a true teacher can ever give their students.

Teacher Leaders' Influence on the Attitude of the Students

A leader always has convictions to achieve his/her life's vision. These convictions can be easily followed or adapted by the students. If the conviction of the leader is to face the challenges of life without any fear, automatically the followers, even though they are fearful, will develop refreshing boldness to face any challenges.

Teacher Leaders' Influence on the Moral Behaviour

The ethics of a leader can sway those who follow him/her—either directly, through the corporate values that are encouraged through his/her leadership, or through his/her policies. If the leader is a high-ranking official over a nation, his morals can permeate an entire culture. You may come from a country in which the leaders have tremendous gifts, communicate well, and are competent in various leadership techniques—but are lacking in ethical convictions.

Many leaders do not take responsibility for their actions. They feel that they should experience no consequence when they betray the trust of their constituents, their employees, their families, or the public. Such an attitude and behaviour do not go unnoticed by followers, so many people begin to think, 'He's a leader, and he did such and such a thing and got away with it, so I can do it too!' That is why it is vital for leaders to recognise and assess the values they currently hold and to establish or re-establish ethical principles that they will commit to stand upon. We will explore this process in the next few chapters.

Teacher Leaders' Influence on the Dedication of the Students

Dedication is a key element in teacher leadership because teaching is not an easy task. It requires a lot of commitment to be a teacher, as it takes a great deal of time and effort to renew them every other day. The teachers need to update and educate themselves on a daily basis to lead their students. So, commitment is the key element for a follower to ascertain and to be influenced by such a commitment, and ultimately, the follower will follow them. The commitment seen in a teacher inspires the students to march towards their life vision. If a teacher-leader sticks to the principles and convictions, the students will also join them.

Teacher leaders' influence on the future of the students

The influence of a leader who has commitment, convictions, and principles can lead the students to a future that they might not have dreamed of in their lives. Many students enter their school studies and higher education without any dream. They are happy just to pursue a degree for the sake of their parents, friends, society, and status. It is the responsibility of each and every teacher-leader to help each and every student identify their true potential and teach them to use their potential for a good cause. When the hidden potential is identified in a student, they become a blessing to society.

Whether you like it or not, teachers, you're the foundation of your students. A building is only as secure as its foundation. A building can have a number of problems. But if a crack is discovered in the foundation of a building, it doesn't matter how nice the interior is; the building will need serious repair, and then no one can use it. As teachers, we need to be careful not to allow any cracks in our character. If you see a crack developing, fix it immediately. Do not let it get any bigger, or the whole structure may collapse. You may think that character lapses affect only you, but they also affect those entrusted to your protection, teaching, and care. Evaluate the current state of your character and take steps to correct what you see. In doing so, you will strengthen your students.

Thought to Ponder

Every teacher needs to improve,
not because they are not good enough,
but because they can be EVEN BETTER

–Dylan Wiliam

Teacher-Leader – a Teacher and a Cultivator

Leadership is about vision and responsibility, not power.

–Seth Berkley

Have you ever wondered why teachers always correct their students? Because they desire to give input. A teacher-leader feels as if they are responsible for the progress of their class. Therefore, they give instructions, advice, and counsel. As a teacher-leader, don't just tell your students to do this or do that. Don't do this or don't do that. Show them how to do it. Watch your life and make sure you keep your word. Some teachers tell their students to be honest, but then they call off work when they are not sick. You cannot teach something unless you are an example of it yourself. A good teacher-leader is one who teaches by example. A teacher-leader is responsible for teaching the unknown to the student followers. It will take great determination and self-sacrifice to prepare your followers to become an influential force in society.

Teach to Empower Your Students

Teacher leadership never exists for itself. It exists for the purpose of guiding others to have a better future, to help them grow in more ways, to help them improve themselves, and to inspire them to believe that anything is possible. People are positively influenced by leadership, which sets standards for them and instils in them a genuine belief in their own capacity for greatness. Student empowerment and value recognition are fostered by teacher leadership, which also cultivates the leader's attitude towards the students. The empowerment of students is a priority for teacher leadership, which commits time, money, effort, and experience.

Teach to Uplift Your Students

Teacher leadership is mentoring, identifying, developing, training, and preparing your students. As teacher leaders, this is one of your primary contributions to the world. Imagine you are a teacher-leader now. You are in your leadership spot, pursuing the vision and carrying out the plan. You really seem to know your purpose, and you have an extraordinary gift in this arena of teacher leadership. Don't get comfortable; it is time to start preparing your students for leadership in different areas. Teacher leaders do not maintain followers. They produce leaders. Teacher leaders believe that leadership potential resides in everyone around them. They create an environment for that leadership to blossom. The heart of a teacher-leader is not just serving one's gift but also helping the students to find their prepared places, to discover their gifts and strengths, and to give them an opportunity to develop. As a teacher-leader, you create an environment for your students to find their authority. You have the authority in your area of gifting. So, as a teacher-leader, your job is to help your students find their area of authority so that they can go and serve the world.

A TEACHER-LEADER IS A CULTIVATOR

Teacher leaders need to fulfil their responsibility as cultivators of their students' lives. To cultivate means to make something better than when you first received it. If a teacher-leader receives their students to work with, they should never end up with just what they were given. When the teacher-leader has completed their work with their students, it should be multiplied, more effective, and fruitful. Teacher leaders are not just teachers; they are developers. Any teacher-leader who wants to be a real leader will appreciate their responsibility to make everything around them better. Teacher leadership is not about making yourself better; it's all about making our students' lives better through selfless efforts.

Teacher-Leader – A Cultivator of His Work, Talents and Skills

There lived a farmer in a small kingdom. He was very talented and skillful. He always desired to increase his resources by applying his knowledge and understanding. He knew that farming was his job, and he was good at coming up with plans to get a lot of crops and make money someday. He decided to solve the water crisis in his kingdom, so he studied a lot of books, spoke with learned people, and then got to work implementing the solutions on his own farm. He advised other farmers to do so, but all others laughed at him and mocked him for what he was doing during the rainy season. It rained cats and dogs. Finally, the farmer's strategies worked as he collected enough water from the rain in his rain harvesting system. The summer started gradually; the water level in the pond and the well dried up in the scorching sun. Every other farmer approached this farmer for help. Now they realised and regretted their mistakes. Now, the whole kingdom has decided to use this rain harvesting technique to save more water for the next summer.

My dear friends, just think about this farmer and his talents. He used them to maximise his yield and influenced others to do the same. Don't we have different talents? Do we want to hide them or use them for the welfare and betterment of our students? If this farmer had not used his talents and multiplied them, he would also have suffered the summer like other farmers. If a person is still working at what he was working at ten years ago and has not improved at all, there's something wrong. Every part of society needs development. If we have real teacher leaders around us, we could see that development in society. Teacher leaders should be cultivators of their work, talents, or skills, not by hiding them but by multiplying them and making them fruitful for society through their student followers.

Teacher Leaders as a Cultivator of Their Students

A teacher-leader's main responsibility is to cultivate their students. They should provide a good learning environment for their personal and career growth. Teachers should build up their students rather than tear them down with their own hands.

Don't call your students stupid, idiots, useless, or worthless. They are your followers. You need to nurture them so they will grow and yield fruit in the right season. When your students go wrong, firmly but gently correct them.

A teacher-leader should help their students to discover their gifts and talents. They should affirm their accomplishments and tell them what they can become in life. Sometimes, as teachers, we walk around with specific pictures in our minds of who we want our students to be, and when they don't meet our expectations, we tend to become very frustrated. The perfect student whom you are looking for does not exist. It is your job to cultivate your students. You should help them to yield fruit and multiply, but not tear them down when they do not meet your expectations. Let me say a word to all the teacher leaders, including me. When a young, fresh student comes into your presence, they should leave a better person than when they came.

Thought to Ponder

If your actions inspire others to dream more, learn more,
do more and become more, you are a leader.

—John Quincy Adams

Be a Person of Values

When values, thoughts, feelings, and actions are in alignment, a person becomes focused, and character is strengthened.

—John C. Maxwell

Rocks are cheap because they are easily available, but diamonds are expensive because they are rare. To make yourself valuable, you need to be unique; you should be remembered for something unique that you have contributed to society. Gold is not valued when it lies in the mines in the dust, but once it is extracted from the mine and made to undergo different processes in the refinery, it becomes valuable or more expensive; likewise, a teacher-leader should focus on making the students valuable to society by producing quality leaders. The following are real-life examples of important leaders who have made themselves valuable.

➢ **Helen Keller** was a girl from a small Alabama town who, due to an illness, lost her sight and hearing before she was two years old. Yet, she became an internationally known lecturer, an author of more than ten books, and a powerful advocate for the rights of the physically disabled. She received the

Presidential Medal of Freedom, and her book, *The Story of My Life*, is still available in more than fifty languages.

➤ **Mother Teresa** was a teacher and nun from Macedonia who decided to devote her life to caring for the destitute in India. Yet, in her compassion and determination to help others, she became an international leader, served as an inspiration for millions, and was awarded the Nobel Peace Prize.

➤ **David**, an insignificant shepherd boy who was considered the least in his family, has his place in history as the greatest king the nation of Israel has ever produced.

Teacher Leaders Who Have Contributed to the World of Education:

There are many teachers who have contributed to the development of the students to become visionary leaders. Teachers have made great changes in education; one such person was the Moravian theologian and educational reformer John Amos Comenius. He was a Czech educational reformer and the discoverer of 'Practical Education,' which is the most remarkable contribution to the field of education imparted during that time. He is considered the 'Father of Modern Education.' He was the first educator to discover and implement the usage of pictures in textbooks and also perceived it as a universal concept of education. He believed that education should originate in the earliest days of adolescence and continue for the entire lifetime. Comenius also believed that every child – boy or girl, rich or poor, skillful or mentally obstructed – needs a rightful education. For him, every educational limitation was a prime hindrance to mankind's progress. As a consequence, he took a stand to eliminate these limitations by writing a number of excellent textbooks.

Teacher Leaders' Influence on the Student Followers:

A leader should live a life to inspire others. If the leader can't make any difference in the life of the follower, he/she is not leading; they are just taking a walk. There are many teachers who have influenced the students in many ways by being responsible for bringing transformation in their lives. In recent years, there has been a real emotional story about a young teacher who went viral on social media. Mr G. Bhagawan, a 28-year-old teacher who teaches English at a Government School in Tiruvallur district, influenced the whole school by the concern he had shown towards the students. The students engulfed him in hugs and tears, exhibited their love and affection towards the teacher, and refused to accept his transfer order. Mr Bhagawan, too, was crying as much as his students. The pictures of this emotional moment were published in the media, and the students' gestures moved even the bureaucracy.

Mr Bhagawan was transferred to the Government High School in Arungulam near Tiruttani – but this deployment was on hold for ten days. Parents, too, supported the children who decided that they would not attend school on a particular day to demonstrate that they were against the government's decision to transfer Mr Bhagawan. They were hugging and crying and clutching the teacher's foot, refusing to let him go. Watching them, students fostered a parental bond with Mr Bhagawan and hence expressed their emotions after hearing about his transfer. Students have been reported as saying that though many teachers have left the school in the past, they have not felt this sad for any of them. When the teacher was asked about how he influenced them, he said that he had tried his best to interact with students beyond just academics. He used to narrate stories, understand their family background, talk to them about their future, and show them things via the projector.

Three Phases of Life Development to Make Yourself Valuable

In order to make ourselves valuable, we need to understand the different stages and their importance in life. The true nature of teacher leadership is to make them valuable by understanding the phases of development. When a teacher makes himself/herself valuable, it's easy for them to inspire their students to become valuable.

1. The Dependent Stage

The dependent stage is the first stage of making yourself valuable. You rely on something or someone in the dependent stage for your existence or survival, like a tree whose root is rooted in the ground or a human embryo that is rooted in a mother's womb. From creation, it is designed to be this way: to be attached to a source to begin its life. As a teacher-leader, you need to attach to a source of knowledge to become a perfect leader, so don't detach yourself from the source until you identify your real potential.

2. The Independent Stage

In our own lives, we have experienced this independence. We depend on our parents at the dependence stage, but when we grow, we detach ourselves from our parents and have our own identity and individuality. In the previous stage, we saw that a tree is attached to the soil, and an embryo is attached to a womb for its survival. Once the embryo is mature, it is detached from the womb. When a tree produces fruit from the nutrition of the soil, the fruit ripens and falls to the ground and starts to become an individual plant. This stage is important in a teacher-leader's life to realise what they are good at. When you figure out how you can be a good leader, you'll be able to stand out as a unique teacher-leader.

3. The Interdependent Stage

Furthermore, a person can simply work with others when they identify themselves. A person cannot live an independent life without having the support of others or without being supported by others. After the country gains independence, it is the job of every teacher-leader to help society continue to grow and change by making new leaders. This is the stage where the teacher creates an ecosystem within the classroom, where you can influence 50 to 60 students by understanding their cultural backgrounds and behaviours. A teacher's behaviour influences a student's behaviour as well. Making yourself valuable is, therefore, inextricably linked to making your student follower a valuable person.

The three stages are important for a teacher-leader to make themselves valuable:

➢ **Dependent** – Depend on your source of knowledge and understanding.

➢ **Independent** – Identifying who you are.

➢ **Interdependent** – Contributing your gifts for the betterment of your followers.

Thought to Ponder

Good teachers are the reason why ordinary students dream to do extraordinary things.

The Art of Producing a Potential Leader

Leaders aren't born, they are made. And they are made just like anything else, through hard work. And that's the price we'll have to pay to achieve that goal or any goal.

—*Vince Lombardi*

True leadership must lead to change; that change should transform itself into social betterment. Teachers, as leaders, should focus on changing their environment. You cannot be a leader if you do not bring changes to your environment. As a teacher, if you are not trying to change the students' mentality and bring transformation in their lives, you are not leading; you are just managing what is in your hand. Teachers must help their students identify their inner potential to bring transformation to society. True teacher leadership is always committed to serving the students to improve their lives.

Teacher leadership is the designated position to lead the leader of the future who is going to carry on the work of leadership. A teacher leader's success is measured by the leaders produced by them in different fields. They create future leaders by sharing their knowledge, experience, skills, expertise, and resources with them. Leadership is not about leading one generation since it's an ongoing process. If you sow the right leadership attitude in the minds of your student followers, it will pass down to several generations through you. Teacher leaders are never worried or afraid of the successful development of those whom they are leading. They rejoice when their student followers develop into leaders and become greater and more effective than they once were. To lead the leader, the teacher should understand the importance of leading the followers and actively preparing them to become leaders in different domains. An important measure of your teacher leadership effectiveness is the followers being productive in their domain, even in your absence. Since the purpose of teacher leadership is to inspire the students to exercise their leadership capacity, we need to understand that the purpose of teacher leadership is to produce a more effective generation of leaders by identifying, developing, and refining the hidden leader in every student follower. If you are going to be an effective leader, you must prepare yourself to produce effective leaders for society.

Discover your Hidden Potential

The potential is a dormant ability that is not used but is present inside each and every human. A teacher leader has the responsibility of helping the student followers to identify his/her potential to be successful in their lives. Many students, without knowing their capability, live below their potential. When the student leaders are identified at the right time, regrets in life can be avoided. A teacher's role is to help them identify their potential. A teacher can help in identifying the potential of the student followers to discover their true self. This self-discovery helps the student followers to live a purposeful life.

Focus on Attitude Change

Attitude is the result of our belief system. Whatever we believe, whether it's true or not, becomes our attitude. It is the same with the student followers; when you, as a teacher leader, take responsibility to bring transformation in your student followers, work it out from their belief system. There are things to be unlearned by us as well as the students to bring changes in the attitude. For example, many of the students have the misconception that they are not leaders; this is the result of their belief system. The belief system of a student turns into their attitude, and the attitude produces the confidence level in them. When the student follower has a negative attitude, his confidence level will be low because he/she will always believe that they cannot. Whenever a teacher leader asks a student to do something, the first reply will be, 'I can't do it,' 'I don't know about it,' they never come up with positive words like 'I will try,' 'I will learn.' This negative as well as the positive attitude is the result of the belief system. So, the teacher should help the students to understand that it is only their belief system that blocks the way to becoming a successful leader.

During the rainy season, it is very difficult to drive a car without the help of the wipers at the front. Every time the wiper moves faithfully, it cleans the windshield of the car countless times and sweeps the water away, helping the drivers to see better what's ahead of them. Likewise, we should make our students understand that there is a life beyond what they see through the blurred mind. Every time they make a move in life, they need to wipe off the blocks to have a clear view of their future. The right attitude is one of the most important qualities the students should possess to become future leaders in their domain.

Help Followers Access Their Gifts and Abilities

Identifying gifts and abilities is important for anyone who wants to become a leader. Many abilities are dormant inside the human mind until they are explored. Some people have the capability to identify their potential by exploring themselves by reading books, collecting information, and understanding their nature through trial and error. However, the majority of the student followers need motivation or inspiration to identify their inner abilities. Teachers have an important responsibility to help their students identify their abilities. The teacher-leader can monitor the way of thinking, behaviour, and character of their student followers closely to help them to access their gifts.

Once upon a time, there lived a monk who had a few disciples. This monk used to give different work to different disciples and monitor how they performed their work. Each day was the routine in the monastery. One fine morning, a disciple asked the monk: "Why today have I been asked to go into the village to teach the children for this week? I don't know how to manage them. I don't know how to deal with them, so I request you to send someone else on my behalf." The monk gently replied, "My dear son, it's not the custom of the monastery to allocate work based on your requirements." This young man was clueless and did not know what to do. He enquired with everyone in the monastery about the children of the village; everyone who had previously visited the village gave very bad feedback. This young disciple did not know what to do now; anyway, he went into the village to meet the children. The children were ready to see who was going to teach them for that week. As soon as he saw the children, he was frightened. He approached them and greeted them, but none of them replied. He did not know what to do as he stared into the eyes of the children. He paused for a few minutes and closed his eyes in fear.

The children closely monitored his reactions. The disciple deeply thought about what he could do best; he thought about all the different work he did every day; nothing was fulfilling to him. Suddenly, he realised the good times he shared with his other friends in the monastery where he made his friends feel happy at night by telling different creative stories. That struck him as being good! So, he opened his eyes and made the students sit, but they didn't listen to him. On the spur of the moment, he started to explain a story in his own way. In another minute, all the students were silenced, and they started listening to him. At the end of the class, the children felt very happy, and the disciple was extremely happy and thoroughly satisfied. He then returned to the monastery in the evening. Everyone visited the monk to report on their work, and at that time, this young disciple explained what happened in the village. He was excited and happy to explain how he taught the students. Now, the monk asked him, "Will you continue going to the village to teach the children?" He smiled and said, 'yes.' Then the monk asked 'why?'

The disciple replied, "I am more satisfied with what I did today than any other work I did in the past." For the next few weeks, the disciple visited the children in the village and taught them ethical and moral values through different stories in his own way. The children awaited him each day and never accepted new teachers.

Prepare the Followers to Serve Their Gifts

Each person in this world is created by God with a distinct gift or skill. It is important to believe that we are created with unique and inherent gifts, abilities, and talents. I would like to give you an example of talent from the book of Matthew in the Bible. A master who was planning to travel entrusted his property to his servants. According to the abilities of each man, one servant received five talents, the second received two, and the third received only one. Talent was an amount of money. Upon returning home, the master asked the three of his servants to give an account of the talents he entrusted to them. The first and the second servants explained that they each put their talents to work and doubled the value of the property with which they were entrusted; each servant was rewarded. The third servant, however, had merely hidden his talent by burying it in the ground and was punished by his master. Consequently, if a talent, skill, or ability is not used appropriately, it will not be rewarded.

It's important to make the students understand that they should make use of the given talents effectively to produce and reproduce continually.

Train Them to Effectively Use the Resources

In administrative and coordinative duties, a leader must always closely monitor the 'big three' – personnel, finances, and planning. True leadership builds effective managerial teams and organises people's diverse gifts and talents to maximise their contribution to the whole. Leaders know the strengths and weaknesses of others and use wisdom when assigning them to particular teams. Effective leaders are also good stewards of the physical and financial resources for which they are responsible. They know how to use them in the best interests of the vision and can make them productive so that they yield good returns. In both the above areas, it is necessary to plan your resources, both short-term and long-term. What is needed now to further the vision? What will be needed next year and in years to come? To become a leader, you must be able to know what resources you have, what resources you still need, and how to use them most effectively.

Train Them to Be Faithful in Their Purpose

True leadership possesses a deep dedication to personal discipline. Personal discipline incorporates self-imposed standards for the sake of achieving noble goals and aspirations that are more important than personal pleasure. Leadership focuses on self-sacrifice for the sake of service rather than on personal comfort and indulgence. It defers present gratification for future goals. Leadership shuns mediocrity for the pursuit of excellence. It imposes restrictions on itself in order to achieve a greater alternative. Leadership involves moulding oneself in order to obtain what is best. Leaders make decisions cognisant of the consequences and their impact on desired goals. In essence, leadership disciplines its decisions based on its dedication to a determined destiny. Leaders control their decisions. That's high discipline. Why did Corrie ten Boom, after reaching the age of fifty, decide to risk her life to protect persecuted Jews in her native Holland during World War II when she could have lived a quiet life? It was self-discipline based on her integrity not to compromise the value of life. Again, leadership never compromises vision for the sake of gaining popularity. Those who practise leadership are willing to walk alone until the crowd catches up. To become a leader, you must learn to discipline your life according to the goals and objectives of your purpose.

Teach to Empower Others

The main purpose of the teacher-leader is to empower the student followers. This attitude of empowering others is to be taught to the student followers because leadership never exists for itself; it exists for the purpose of guiding others to a better future, enabling them to develop in greater ways, helping them to improve themselves, and inspiring them to believe that anything is possible. Leadership sets standards for people and influences them positively, giving them hope and deep conviction about their own abilities to achieve greatness. To become a leader, you must be committed to empowering others.

Teach Leadership Values

The value of faithfulness, the value of resources, the value of integrity, the value of responsibility, the value of self-discipline, and the value of passing it on are the important values a student follower should learn under the training of each teacher-leader.

The greatest investment in leadership is not in things but in people. Even though we are necessarily involved in a variety of activities to fulfil our visions, we as leaders must ask, "Whom am I investing in to produce better leaders in the future and after my generation?" Let me re-emphasise that the most valuable investment anyone can make is in another person, not in a piece of property or equipment. People who intend to extend their lives through projects will ultimately fail. The purpose of leadership is to inspire every follower to become a leader and fulfil his potential.

There is leadership potential in every person. I encourage you to set your life on a course of leadership training that will enable you to become an exceptional leader for your generation to emulate. The realisation of your leadership potential is tied to your willingness to commit, refine, develop, and incorporate the characteristics of leadership in your life. You must commit to becoming a leader. Many people will merely continue to sit at home, hoping that someone will come along and promote them to something better. They will sit for years, waiting—and they will die waiting. You can't afford to let that happen to you.

Our world is suffering from a lack of leadership, but you can help change this situation. You have within you the ability to become a change agent in your time. Don't wait for someone else to take responsibility for the future. Rise up from the seat of a follower and enter the school of leadership, for it is God's will that you become a leader and lead others to their fullest potential in Him. Settle for nothing less than your best. If you accept this challenge, then read this book again until you are filled with the desire and knowledge to lead others to leadership. Be available and say, "I want to do something on this earth." Discover God's purpose and vision for your life. Then, step out in faith and do it!

Thought to Ponder

"The greatest leader is not necessarily the one who does the greatest things. He is the one that gets the people to do the greatest things."

–Ronald Reagan

THINKING IT OVER

Have you accepted the cost of teacher leadership? List out the areas in which you need development.

THINKING IT OVER---

ACTING ON IT

Write down great thoughts about the area of improvement and repeat them aloud to yourself daily and practise it daily.

TEACHER LEADERSHIP

THE GREATEST OF ALL LEADERSHIP

About the Author

Dr. S. Smilee Bose was born in the serene town of Nagercoil, Kanyakumari District, Tamil Nadu. As early as her school days, she had already earned a name for herself as a brilliant speaker.

She is a passionate teacher and a phenomenal orator who always leaves a favourable impression, educating and impacting young listeners for a lifetime. Her book, *Leader of Leaders*, educates readers about successful leadership, giving them more self-assurance to achieve important goals in life. With almost a decade of teaching and research experience, the author has, to her credit, been a blogger, quote writer, YouTuber, motivational speaker, and keynote speaker.

The author has presented and published many research papers at national and international levels. She was honoured with the title 'Best Professor' instituted by the International Education Awards 2022.

At present, she works as an Associate Professor & Head of the Department of Corporate Secretaryship at St. Peter's Institute of Higher Education and Research, Avadi, Chennai.